SPEL

Mary Sidley

POND VIEW BOOKS

First published in Great Britain 1994 by
Hawthorns Publications Limited
Pond View House, Otford, Kent

Reprinted 1994

ISBN 1 871044 55 3

Preface

This book is designed to help children of primary school age, or older students having difficulty with spelling, not only to spell correctly but also to gain some idea of word-building and the 'rules' of spelling.

It starts with a range of quite simple words and exercises and gradually progresses to more difficult words which are commonly misspelt by people of all ages.

The importance of correct spelling cannot be too strongly emphasised, not least in the light of the National Curriculum and testing at all key stages. Each page of this book should represent a helpful challenge.

Mary Sidley

Contents

Simple word changes	pages 1-5
Words which sound the same or similar	pages 6-9
Words commonly misspelt	pages 10-13
Ough words	page 14
Wh words	page 15
Words that begin, or end, with a silent letter	pages 16-17
Spelling changes from singular to plural	pages 18-20
Word-building and changes in spelling	pages 21-22
More words commonly misspelt	pages 23-25
Nouns and verbs – spelling changes	pages 26-27
Words commonly confused	pages 28-29
More difficult words to spell	page 30
Puzzle pages	pages 31-37
Puzzle page answers	pages 38-39
Notes	page 40

Simple word changes

Here, to start with, are some simple 3-lettered words which are easy for you to spell.

Notice how they can be changed into quite different words by adding **e**.

fat	–	fate
bit	–	bite
not	–	note
can	–	cane
din	–	dine
mad	–	made
hid	–	hide
rod	–	rode
bar	–	bare
rag	–	rage

Can you think of any other 3-lettered words which are changed in this way by adding **e**?

Try to make a list of words of your own.

When you add **ing** to a word ending in **e**, you usually drop the **e**.

For example:	come	–	coming
	bite	–	biting
	like	–	liking

Can you complete the following list in the same way?

hide hid___

write

bathe

hope

dine

shine

wake

smile

hike

file

ride

Some words double the last letter before adding **ing**.

For example:	dig	–	digging
	wag	–	wagging
	shop	–	shopping
	drip	–	dripping

Complete the following sentences by using double letters:

1. The girl was ski . . ing with a rope.
2. The plumber mended the dri . . ing tap.
3. The dog was be . . ing for its food.
4. The sportsman was jo . . ing along the path.
5. Little Miss Muffet was si . . ing on a tuffet.
6. The tennis player was hi . . ing the ball hard
7. The gardener was cli . . ing the hedge.

In the same way, the final letter is doubled before adding **ed**.

For example:	shop	–	shopped
	knit	–	knitted
	rub	–	rubbed
	tin	–	tinned

Complete these sentences with double-lettered words:

1. The car ski . . ed on the icy road.
2. The present was wra . . ed in brown paper.
3. The children dro . . ed coins into the wishing well.
4. The dog wa . . ed its tail in excitement.
5. The cricketer ba . . ed well in the match.
6. The man ste . . ed quickly across the road.
7. The woman sli . . ed on the polished floor.

Make sure you know the difference between **ick** and **ike**, **ack** and **ake** words.

Here are some examples:

lick	–	like
pick	–	pike
back	–	bake
lack	–	lake
rack	–	rake
sack	–	sake

Complete the following sentences by using words set out above:

1. My mother is going to b . . . a cake today.
2. What time do you come b . . . from school?
3. The water in this l . . . is very deep.
4. After eating, the cat will l . . . its paws.
5. The man decided to r . . . his lawn.
6. Tom won the s . . . race.
7. It was time to p . . . the apples from the tree.

Words which sound the same or similar

There are words which are often confused, such as: **where**, **wear** and **were**.

For example: This is **where** I live.

What clothes are you going to **wear**?

There **were** thirty children in the class.

Make up three sentences of your own using the above words.

Other words which are often misspelt are **there** and **their**; there means *in that place* and their means *belonging to them.*

(Remember that both words begin with th**e**)

Choose the correct word, **there** or **their**, to complete these sentences:

1. I put the books over th . . .
2. Th . . . are no more biscuits in the tin.
3. The boys wore th . . . football boots.
4. She does not go th . . . on Saturdays.
5. Th . . . house is two miles from the nearest town.

Don't forget that **they're** is short for **they are**.

For example: **They're** going home tomorrow.

They're shows the use of the apostrophe to make two words into one. The apostrophe is placed where at least one letter has been left out.

Examples:			
	I'll	–	I will
	isn't	–	is not
	can't	–	cannot

Complete the following list, putting the apostrophe in the correct place. The first word is done for you:

do not	–	don't
could not	–	
I am	–	
they will	–	
has not	–	
have not	–	
we would	–	
shall not	–	
you are	–	
who is	–	

Remember the difference between **whose** and **who's**.

Whose means *belonging to whom*, as in: **Whose** books are these?

Who's means *who is*, as in: **Who's** going to the cinema today?

In the same way, it is important not to mix up **are** and **our**.

Are is the plural of *is* and *our* means *belonging to us*.

For example: We **are** going on holiday tomorrow.

We keep **our** toys in a cupboard.

Complete the following sentences:

1. Dad gives us ___ pocket money every Saturday.

2. Where ___ the Houses of Parliament?

Remember that **hour** sounds the same as **our** and **hour** refers to time.

For example: There **are** sixty minutes in an **hour**.

Many more words sound the same but are spelt differently.

For example: pear (a fruit)

pair (two of anything)

pare (to peel a fruit)

Other examples are:

fair	–	fare
hair	–	hare
maid	–	made
sail	–	sale
fir	–	fur
bare	–	bear
tail	–	tale
through	–	threw

Choose any eight of the above words and write sentences to show their meaning.

For example: The rabbit's **fur** is soft and thick.

He **threw** the ball high into the air.

The **maid** cleaned the hotel bedroom.

Underline in each sentence the word you have used from the list.

Words commonly misspelt

Words which are often misspelt are: **though**, **through** and **thought**.

Make sure you know each word's meaning and spell it correctly in the following sentences:

1. The cows were herded th . . . . . the gate into the field.
2. I have th . . . . . of a present for your birthday.
3. We will go to play football even th . . . . it is raining.
4. The cricket ball went right th . . . . . the window and into the room.
5. The boy was chosen to play football for England th . . . . he was only seventeen.
6. The children th . . . . . they would go for a hike in the country.

Other words spelt like **thought** are:

ought

bought

fought

nought

brought

Do not muddle them with **aught** words like:

caught

taught

daughter

naughty

haughty

Write ten sentences using each of the above words to show their meaning.

For example: You **ought** to look both ways before crossing the road.

You may need to use a dictionary.

Some **ight** words are often misspelt, for example, **site** for **sight**.

Fit the following **ight** words to the correct phrase or sentence in the list opposite them:

tight	two weeks
bright	to make someone afraid
delight	how tall someone is
lightning	She wears glasses because her _______ isn't good.
frighten	These shoes are too _______ .
fortnight	a journey by aeroplane
height	strong and powerful
flight	The sun's rays are very _______ .
eyesight	Thunder always follows _______ .
mighty	joy or great pleasure
alight	opposite of left
right	on fire

Remember that in words like **queen** and **quiz**, **q** is always followed by **u**, and be careful not to confuse **quite** and **quiet**.

For example: This answer is not **quite** right.

It is very **quiet** and peaceful by the river.

How many other words can you think of that begin with **qu**?

You may use a dictionary for this and make sure you spell each word correctly.

Ough words

Many words ending with **ough** sound quite different from each other.

Can you fit each of the following **ough** words to its correct meaning in the list below?

WORD	MEANING
bough	plenty
cough	not smooth
dough	a branch of a tree
rough	even if
tough	a sound from the throat
though	from one side to the other
through	not easily broken
enough	a mixture of flour, fat and water
plough	drinking-place for horses
trough	turn over the soil

Wh words

Some **wh** words can be confused.

why

what — In all except **who** and **whom** the **w/wh** is sounded.

where

when

which

who — **Who** and **whom** sound as if they begin with **h**, as does the word **whole**.

whom

These words can all ask questions. For example: Where are you going?

Write sentences using the following **wh** words:

whisper

whether

whip

whistle

Don't confuse **whether** with **weather**; whether means *if*.

Remember the difference between **which** and **witch**.

Which book will you choose?

The **witch** rode on her broomstick.

Words that begin, or end, with a silent letter

As well as **who** and **whom**, there are other words which start with a silent **w**, such as the following:

write

wrong

wrist

wrap

wren

wring

wreck

wreath

Complete the following sentences with a word from the above list.

1. The _______ is the smallest bird in Britain.
2. You have given the _______ answer.
3. In last night's storm there was a ship _______ .
4. She wore a bangle round her _______ .
5. A _______ of holly hung on the front door.
6. I am going to _______ a letter.
7. You must _______ the water out of clothes after washing them.
8. Make sure you _______ the present carefully.

Other words start with a silent **k**.

For example: knock

know

knee

kneel

knife

knave

How many other words can you think of that begin with a silent **k**?

These words have a silent **b**: crumb, climb, lamb.

Can you think of more words with a silent **b**?

Here are some clues to help you:

1. You use this to do your hair.
2. Part of your hand
3. This will explode when it is dropped.
4. Unable to speak
5. He works with things such as pipes and taps.

Spelling changes from singular to plural

Many singular words change their spelling completely in the plural. (*Singular* means *one* and *plural* means *more than one*.)

Those words ending in **f** or **fe** change to **ves**.

For example:	knife	–	knives
	loaf	–	loaves

Can you complete the list below?

SINGULAR	PLURAL
elf	
scarf	
wife	
half	
self	
calf	
shelf	
leaf	
life	

Usually, words ending in **y** change to **ies** in the plural.

For example:	baby	–	babies
	fly	–	flies
	try	–	tries

Complete the following list:

SINGULAR	PLURAL
lady	
fairy	
dairy	
diary	
berry	
spy	
lorry	
library	
sentry	
cherry	
country	

Most words ending in **ey**, however, simply add **s** in the plural.

Here are some of them:

key	–	keys
monkey	–	monkeys
donkey	–	donkeys
valley	–	valleys
money	–	moneys

What is the singular of the following words?

SINGULAR	PLURAL
	diaries
	journeys
	daisies
	jockeys
	alleys
	worries
	abbeys
	countries

Word-building and changes in spelling

When **full** is added to a word, it drops the final **l**.

For example: **careful** not carefull

Can you fit the following words ending in **ful** into the sentences below?

beautiful

tearful

wonderful

useful

plentiful

faithful

cheerful

powerful

1. The dog is considered to be man's f_______ friend.
2. That tractor has a very p_______ engine.
3. Having lost her toy, the child was t_______.
4. There was a p_______ amount of food at the party.
5. What a b_______ picture that is!
6. From the hilltop you can see a w_______ view.
7. Although she is poor the old lady always looks c_______.
8. It is u_______ to have an umbrella when it is raining.

When **fully** is added to a word, a double **l** is used.

For example:	careful	–	carefully
	awful	–	awfully
	cheerful	–	cheerfully

Complete these sentences by using the correct words from the list following:

1. The servant always served his master f_______.
2. The princess is dressed b_______.
3. In busy traffic you should cross the road very c_______.
4. When in court the witness answered questions t_______.

truthfully

carefully

beautifully

faithfully

More words commonly misspelt

Remember that words like **almost** and **also** are spelt with one **l** and not two.

Write sentences to show the meaning of the following **al** words.

always

altogether

almost

also

alternative

already

although

almighty

You will sometimes see *alright* written with only one **l**. This is generally thought to be incorrect. It should be written as two words:

all right

For example: The teacher said it was **all right** for us to leave school early.

When **ph** appears in a word it sounds like **f**.

Try to learn the following **ph** words and then use each one in a sentence of your own.

You may use a dictionary to help you if necessary.

telephone

photograph

elephant

pheasant

triumphant

phrase

phobia

physiotherapy

pharmacy

atmosphere

phantom

phase

physical

Words containing the letters **ie** are often spelt wrongly. Although, as a rule, **ie** rather than **ei** is used except after **c** (for example, **receive**, there are many exceptions to this rule.

Use the following **ie** words in sentences of your own.

niece	field	believe
thief	piece	handkerchief

Some words containing **ei** are:

seize	neither	weigh	reign	neigh
ceiling	either	eight	foreign	neighbour

Choose the correct word from the above list to fit in the following sentences.

1. Donkeys bray and horses _______ .
2. A prince may one day _______ over his people.
3. Can you speak a _______ language?
4. _______ John nor his sister is at school today.
5. Our _______ has painted the fence between our gardens.
6. The Christmas decorations are hanging from the ______ in the lounge.

Nouns and verbs – spelling changes

Some words change their spelling according to whether they are used as nouns (naming words, such as **advice**) or verbs (doing words, such as **advise**).

For example:

1. I took my mother's **advice** and went to bed early.
2. My tennis coach **advised** me to keep my eye on the ball.

To take another example: **practice** (noun)

practise, **practised** (verb)

1. He is going to football **practice** with the team.
2. I **practise** playing the piano for two hours every day.
3. The choir **practised** singing a new hymn.

In the same way, **licence** is the noun and **license** is the verb.

1. My father bought the car **licence** today.
2. You must **license** your television set.
3. The fisherman was **licensed** to fish in that river.

Complete the following sentences with the correct word, advice, advise, advised, licence, license, licensed, practice, practise or practised:

1. If you do not p_______ every day you will never become perfect.
2. I was a_______ to eat an apple every day.
3. Netball p_______ takes place on Saturday afternoons.
4. I have just bought a car l_______.
5. Our teacher gave us a_______ about cleaning our teeth.
6. The boy who crashed the car was not l_______ to drive it.
7. You have not p_______ the piece that I gave you to learn.
8. If you do not l_______ your television you may be fined.
9. I a_______ my sister as to how she should dress.

Words commonly confused

The words **accept** and **except** are often confused.

Accept means *to take something that is given to you*. For example: Will you **accept** this gift with our thanks?

Except means *leaving out*. For example: All the children **except** John attended the party.

Do not confuse **except** with **expect**.

For example: I **expect** it to be cold in winter.

Some other words beginning with **ex** are:

exactly

examine

exhausted

experiment

exercise

expel

Can you write six sentences to show the meanings of the above six words?

Other words which begin with **exc**, like **except**, are:

exception

excite

exceed

excitement

excess

Using a dictionary to help you, if necessary, complete the following sentences using a word from the above list, including except.

1. Mary was filled with _______ at the thought of her birthday party.
2. With the _______ of February the months of the year have either 30 or 31 days.
3. You must not _______ the speed limit in your car.
4. Every boy _______ John is going to school tomorrow.
5. If you _______ that dog too much he may bite you.
6. The drunken driver had _______ alcohol in his blood.

More difficult words to spell

Now that we have come to the end of the book, here are some more difficult words for you to spell.

The following words are frequently misspelt by adults as well as children. See how many of them you can learn to spell correctly.

because	pursue
separate	coffee
different	cushion
colour	instead
favourite	disappear
empty	farther
benefited	expense
raspberry	scissors
bicycle	remembrance
opposite	February

These are even more difficult words:

parliament
miniature
mischievous
accommodation
disappointment
dissatisfaction

If you can now spell correctly **every** word in this book, go to the top of the class!

Puzzle page

Crossword

Clues

Across

1. A freshwater fish
3. Belonging to us
4. Frozen water
5. Supposing that
7. Drawings, paintings
8. Floor covering
9. Opposite of off
10. Expanse of salt water
12. Used in cricket
13. A fruit

Down

1. A vegetable
2. To make by using long needles
3. A kilogramme __ beans
6. A parent
8. Created
11. I live __ 5, High Street

Puzzle page

Words which are *similar* or *opposite* in meaning – can you complete the following?

small	little	large
timid		
pretty		
rich		
wide		
moist		
courageous		
rapid		
enormous		
afraid		
sad		

Can you find the following jumbled animals?

roesh	mlba	emcla	anpda
btriab	grtei	agto	oykmen
ogd	ltehepna	onil	frgfeia

Puzzle page

Father is about to light a Catherine-wheel. Beginning at the fuse, find the words on the wheel and write sentences to illustrate their meaning.

Puzzle page

Treasure trail

Here are some jumbled words, all of which you have come across earlier in this book. Write the words against their numbers below the trail – and see how quickly you can reach the treasure!

1	9
2	10
3	11
4	12
5	13
6	14
7	15
8	16

Puzzle page

Hidden Words

In the square below, reading downwards and straight across, you will find ten words which you have used earlier in the book. Find those words and use each of them in a sentence to show that you know what they mean.

A	X	L	U	T	W	A	L	Q	B
D	I	G	G	I	N	G	M	E	S
V	R	A	R	G	R	Z	U	P	T
I	W	N	J	H	B	A	Q	T	R
C	T	P	G	T	H	O	U	G	H
E	F	A	S	G	E	Y	I	O	I
B	C	I	D	F	I	J	T	Q	K
E	W	R	O	N	G	K	E	X	I
H	K	Q	V	I	H	M	Z	C	N
T	A	U	G	H	T	P	B	L	G

Puzzle page

Step by Step ...

By writing your answers to these clues in the squares on the steps on the next page, work your way from the top to the bottom.

1. Tennis is played on a _______ .
2. When there are a lot of cars on the road there is heavy _______ .
3. The batsman was out when the fielder _______ the ball.
4. There was a _______ in the churchyard.
5. The _______ of the car will stop it.
6. A soft cry.
7. A glass often _______ when it falls to the floor.
8. A kettle of boiling water gives off _______ .
9. Beef and lamb are examples of _______ .
10. There are eleven players in a football _______ .
11. The friends arranged to _______ under the station clock.
12. When it rains heavily we sometimes say that it _______ with rain.

Start here
1
2
3
4
5
6
7
8
9
10
11
12
You've arrived – well done!

Puzzle page answers

Crossword

Accross

1. pike
3. our
4. ice
5. if
7. art
8. mat
9. on
10. sea
12. bat
13. pear

Down

1. potato
2. knit
3. of
6. father
8. made
11. at

Jumbled animals

horse	lamb	camel	panda
rabbit	tiger	goat	monkey
dog	elephant	lion	giraffe

Treasure trail

1. key
2. ride
3. hare or hear
4. hid
5. bite
6. bake
7. rag
8. try
9. threw
10. wren
11. know
12. lorry
13. our
14. also
15. self
16. where

Hidden Words

advice	tight	pair	height
quite	hiking	digging	though
	wrong	taught	

Step by Step ...

1. court
2. traffic
3. caught
4. tomb
5. brakes
6. sob
7. breaks
8. steam
9. meat
10. team
11. meet
12. teems

Notes

Here are some pages for you to copy down any words which you tend to misspell. To help you, add definitions, words with similar meanings, or opposites.